Sid le Chat

First published in United Kingdom 2020

Text copyright ©Caroline Symonds 2020
Illustrations ©Barnaby Booth 2020

The moral rights of the author and the illustrator have been asserted.

ISBN: 978-1-910563-14-4

Printed and bound by Ingram Spark

All rights reserved. No part of this publication can be reproduced, stored in a retrieval system, or transmitted in any form or by any means, electronic, mechanical, photocopying, recording, or otherwise, without the prior permission of the copyright owners.

French nouns are masculine or feminine.

Un chat

Une panthère

(Sid thinks he's a panther! Oh Sid!)

Un = a (masculine)
Une = a (feminine)

Le = the (masculine)
La = the (feminine)

Sid est un chat noir.

Noir means black.

Noire means black too if it describes a feminine noun.

(une panthère noire)

Blanc = white
(Blanche in feminine form)

Gris = grey
(Grise in feminine form)

Cats come in lots of other colours too (but not usually purple or green!)

Can you see that the colour adjective comes after the noun in French?

Sid est un chat noir.

Sid est une panthère noire !!

Sid est un chien noir ?!!
Noooo!!
(Chien means dog.
Cats do not like to be
mistaken for dogs!)

Sid a cinq ans.

In French you 'have' age, so Sid has five years means Sid is five.

'a' means has

Some more numbers

Un = 1 (say 'ahn')
Deux = 2 ('duh')
Trois = 3 ('twa')
Quatre = 4 ('katr')
Cinq = 5 ('sank')
Six = 6 ('seess')
Sept = 7 ('set')
Huit = 8 ('weet')
Neuf = 9 ('nurf')
Dix = 10 ('deess')

That's a lot of Sids!!!! Eeek!!

Sid a un frère et une sœur.

Un frère is a brother.

Une sœur is a sister.

Did you remember that 'a' means has?

Let's look at the rest of the verb 'have':

J'ai – I have
Tu as – You have
Il a – He has
Elle a – She has
Nous avons – we have
Vous avez – you have
Ils ont – They have
Elles ont – they have

(Sid has a lot of attitude! Cheeky Sid!)

Did you see that there are two forms of 'you' and two forms of 'they'?

Tu is used for friends and family.
Vous is more formal and is used when you are talking to more than one person (plural).

Sid uses tu a lot.
He doesn't use vous much.
Cats are not very formal!

Ils means they when there are a group of boys,
or boys and girls.
Elles means they, when you are speaking about a group of girls.

Sid has lots of friends.
(He has a few enemies too!!
Scary Sid!)

Son frère s'appelle Jimmy.

S'appelle means 'is called' or 'calls himself'.

Je m'appelle means: I am called.

Sid's brother is called Jimmy

What are you called?

'Son' means his.
It also means 'her' when the next word is masculine, like frère.

Here are some more masculine possessive words:

Mon = My
Ton = Your
Notre = Our
Votre = Your
Leur = Their

Sid's sister is called Tia.

Sa sœur s'appelle Tia.

'Sa' means his or her when the next word is feminine, like sœur.

Tia thinks Sid is a bit silly when he is acting like a panther!

Here are some more feminine possessive words.

Ma = My
Ta = Your
Notre = Our
Votre = Your
Leur = Their

Ta and ton are used when talking to friends and family.
Votre is formal and plural.

Sid aime le poisson
et Jimmy et Tia aiment le poulet.

$Et = and$

Aime and aiment mean 'like'.

Do you like cats?
I hope so, otherwise Sid may get a bit grumpy with you...

Let's look at the rest of the verb to like:

J'aime – I like
Tu aimes – You like
Il aime – He likes
Elle aime – She likes
Nous aimons – we like
Vous aimez – you like
Ils aiment – They like
Elles aiment – They like

The word aiment is pronounced aime
– you don't say the ent.

Sid est noir.
Jimmy et Tia sont gris.

Remember 'est' from earlier?
'Est' means 'is' when there is one cat.
When there is more than one cat,
use the word 'sont', for 'are'.

Let's look at the rest of the verb to describe being:

Je suis – I am
Tu es – You are
Il est – He is
Elle est – She is
Nous sommes – We are
Vous êtes – You are
Ils sont – They are
Elles sont – They are

Are you good at French? Yes!
Thanks to Sid you are!

Sid mange le poisson pour son petit déjeuner.

Son petit déjeuner = his breakfast

Let's not forget Sid's other meals:

Son déjeuner = his lunch
Son dîner = his dinner
Son goûter = his snack

(Cats like to eat a lot!)

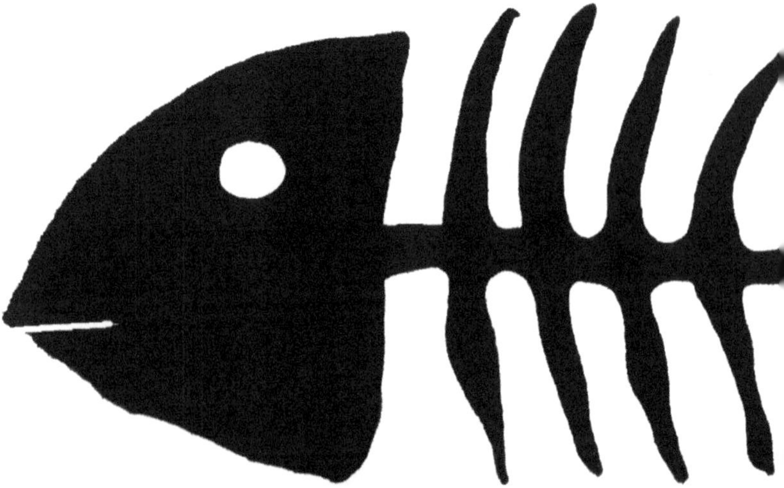

'Mange' means 'eats'.

This verb is formed in exactly the same way as the 'like' verb we looked at.

Je mange – I eat
Tu manges – You eat
Il mange – He eats
Elle mange – She eats
Nous mangeons – We eat
Vous mangez – You eat
Ils mangent – They eat
Elles mangent – They eat

Both of the French verbs to
like and to eat are called
regular 'er' verbs.

Their infinitive form
– how you would read it
in the dictionary – is
aimer and manger.

The way they are formed
is regular and predictable.

Cats like things to be regular
and predictable,
especially their meal times!

Sid is pleased you wanted to learn with him and is proud of you for making it to the end of his little cat-book.

Now it is your turn.

Can you write in French:
Sid is a cat.

How about:

Sid is a black cat.

Now try:

Sid is five years old.

Write:

Sid has a brother and a sister.

Write:

His brother is called Jimmy.

And:

His sister is called Tia.

Now try:

Sid likes fish and
Jimmy and Tia
like chicken.

Write:

Sid is black and
Jimmy and Tia are grey.

Write:

Sid eats fish for his breakfast.

That's the end of Sid's book.
He hopes that he helped you
like French.

Now Sid is going to say
'au revoir'.

That means goodbye.

About the author
Caroline Symonds

Caroline Symonds has liked French since her first encounter with 'je suis'. Unashamed grammar geek, she enjoyed the French language so much she did a degree in it and for many years has been teaching French (and Italian too) to a cast of charismatic students - young, older and middling! This book, her first, aims to use what she has observed about what students usually find tricky when learning French to make basic grammar accessible.

Caroline has been a cat fan, ever since Sid, a previously stray cat, sashayed into her family's life a few years ago and decided that they, or rather their food bowl, could meet his needs!

About the illustrator
Barnaby Booth

When he was at school, Barnaby Booth was so bad at French that he was the only pupil not to take the O' level exam. He's also allergic to cats. And doesn't like drawing much. He's not quite sure how he got talked into doing this, but he says it's been quite good fun and he hopes that you will enjoy the book.

www.ingramcontent.com/pod-product-compliance
Lightning Source LLC
Chambersburg PA
CBHW040418100526
44588CB00022B/2863